Y0-CXG-177

THE LIFE OF WILLIAM SHAKESPEARE

WITHDRAWN
No longer the property of the
Boston Public Library.
Sale of this material benefits the Library.

BOSTON
PUBLIC
LIBRARY

The Life
of
William Shakespeare

BY GILES E. DAWSON

FOLGER BOOKS

Published by
THE FOLGER SHAKESPEARE LIBRARY

Copyright © 1958 by the Folger Shakespeare Library.
All rights reserved.

We are indebted to the Shakespeare Birthplace Trust for permission to
reproduce the photographs in Plates 1-7 and 10-13.

The Folger Shakespeare Library is administered by the Trustees of Amherst
College.

First printing 1958
Second printing 1963
Third printing 1979

AUG - - 1990

LC 79-65979

ISBN 0-918016-06-1

ISBN 0-918016-18-5 (Series)

EGLESTON SQUARE

Printed in the United States of America

PR2899
D3
1979x

WILLIAM SHAKESPEARE was recognized in his own time as the best of the dramatists supplying plays for London's half dozen theatres. *Romeo and Juliet, Richard III,* and *Hamlet* were among the most popular productions on the Elizabethan stage. Still, if the first audience at one of these plays could have been polled after the performance was over, it is not inconceivable that half of them would have been unable to name the author. A generation not blessed with newspapers, magazines, public relations offices, advertising campaigns, or women's clubs neither knew nor cared much about the men who wrote the plays, however excellent the plays might be. No youths pursued Shakespeare with autograph albums; no collector would have given a shilling to acquire the original manuscript of *Hamlet.* Autographs and autograph manuscripts were not valued and not collected. Yet men did talk about Shakespeare and held opinions about him and his writings, and some fifty or sixty persons commented on him or alluded to him in print during the poet's lifetime. Most of these printed allusions, however, are concerned with one or another of Shakespeare's plays or poems; few speak of the poet himself; none furnish details about his private life. This is just what we should expect. People were interested in plays, and to some extent in actors, but not in playwrights.

This characteristically Elizabethan attitude has had the effect of denying to us much knowledge of Shakespeare's personality and his private activities which we might have had if men had written reviews, articles, and books about him. In this kind of biographical obscurity Shakespeare is like all other Elizabethan dramatists and, for that matter, nearly all of his contemporaries, apart from those who achieved great distinction in church or state. Personal letters, diaries, and account books sometimes supply detailed information, but even these are more concerned with business than with personalities. And private papers have been preserved, as a rule, only in the great country houses

1

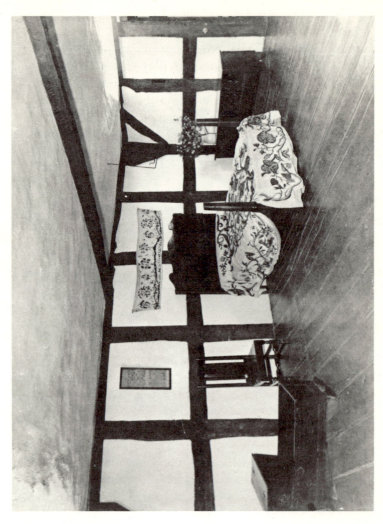

Plate 1. Shakespeare's Birthplace. According to well-founded tradition, Shakespeare was born in this room. Like other upstairs rooms in the house, it is now fitted up with furniture of the sort likely to have been found in the house of a prosperous tradesman such as John Shakespeare in the late sixteenth century.

occupied generation after generation by families of the ruling class, whose private and official affairs had to be recorded and who had ample room for storing old papers. Elizabethan dramatists did not belong to such families, and any private papers they owned or produced have not, with the most trifling exceptions, survived. Those papers that had the best chance of survival were official records of governments, cities, towns, parishes, and corporations. It is mainly from these that our scanty knowledge of the activities and movements of Elizabethan individuals is derived. Parish registers, deeds, tax records, court records, government orders, fiscal documents, wills —all these possessed an obvious value for the future, and provision was made for their preservation. When a private person is married, when he pays his taxes, when he sues his neighbor or is sued by him, when he runs afoul of the law, when he buys or sells real property, when, finally, he dies and is buried—then his name enters the permanent record.

It is so with Shakespeare. What we know about him comes largely from records of the kinds just mentioned. The most important of these are listed below:

1) Stratford-upon-Avon parish register, recording baptisms, marriages, and burials (see Plate 3).
2) The Register of the Bishop of Worcester, containing documents relating to a license for Shakespeare's marriage, 1582.
3) The grant of arms, by the official College of Arms, to John Shakespeare, 1596.
4) A writ of attachment addressed to the sheriff of Surrey, bringing charges against Shakespeare and others, 1596.
5) Documents connected with taxation in London, 1597–1599.
6) Documents connected with the purchase and repair of New Place, 1597–1616.
7) Letters written by or addressed to Richard and Adrian Quiney, mentioning Shakespeare, 1598.
8) A document relating to the holdings of grain by residents of Stratford, including Shakespeare, 1598.

9) Several documents which name Shakespeare as an actor or as a member of the Lord Chamberlain's Men (later the King's Men), the acting company to which Shakespeare belonged.
10) Several documents relating to the joint ownership, by Shakespeare and others, of the Globe and Blackfriars playhouses.
11) Documents concerned with the buying of real property in or near Stratford in 1602.
12) Wills of Thomas Pope and Augustine Phillips (1605), actors and shareholders in the King's Men.
13) Stratford Court of Record documents concerned with the collection by Shakespeare of money owed to him by two fellow townsmen, 1604 and 1608.
14) Documents concerning the lease of Stratford tithes by Shakespeare, 1605.
15) Shakespeare's deposition (Court of Requests) in the suit of Belott v. Mountjoy, 1612.
16) Deeds of the purchase by Shakespeare of a house in Blackfriars, London, 1613.
17) Shakespeare's will, 1616.

The first pertinent entry in the parish register tells us that William, son of John Shakespeare, was baptized on April 26, 1564, a Wednesday. We do not know the date of his birth. The Prayer Book of 1559 urges parents not to defer baptism beyond the Sunday or holy day following the baby's birth. If this was intended to suggest that Sundays and holy days should be preferred for baptisms, no preference for any particular day is observable in the Stratford register in the 1560's. All we can assume about the custom there is that baptism would normally follow birth by no more than a few days. The anniversary of Shakespeare's birth has for some two centuries been celebrated on April 23, a date suggested only by unreliable late tradition, perhaps influenced by the odd but irrelevant fact of his death on April 23, fifty-two years later. It is as likely a date as any other.

Plate 2. Shakespeare's Birthplace. In this half-timbered house, built in the early sixteenth century, Shakespeare was born and spent his earliest years. It was then two separate structures, John Shakespeare's dwelling and his shop. Since 1857, when it was restored, it has been a shrine visited by many thousands of tourists every year.

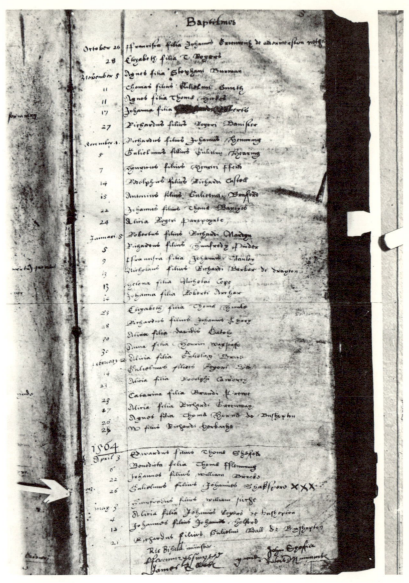

Plate 3. The Parish Register. Under date of April 26, 1564, is the entry of Shakespeare's baptism: "Gulielmus filius Johannes Shakspere." On other pages are entries of his burial and of the baptisms, marriages, or burials of his parents, his brothers and sisters, his wife, his children, his grandchildren. The Register may still be seen in the parish church.

6

John Shakespeare, glover or leatherworker, was a burgess of Stratford—one of the substantial tradesmen elected to the town council. About 1558 he had married Mary, daughter of Robert Arden, a landowning farmer of Wilmcote, not far from Stratford. Of this union were born eight children, of whom William was the third child and the first son.

On Shakespeare's boyhood there is no documentary evidence. His plays and poems abound with passages that might be taken as recollections of the Warwickshire countryside, such as this description of a hunted hare:

> Then shalt thou see the dew-bedabbled wretch
> Turn and return, indenting with the way;
> Each envious brier his weary legs doth scratch,
> Each shadow makes him stop, each murmur stay.

Much of this sort of thing may well reflect in some way Shakespeare's stored-up memories of childhood; it would be remarkable if the experiences of his childhood were not reflected in innumerable ways in his mature work. But it is impossible to read this record now, and we cannot reasonably say that any particular passage had its origin in the recollection of the years in Stratford. We are entitled to suppose that the young Shakespeare spent these years in the usual activities of boyhood. Other boys in Stratford outwardly not very different from him went to school, for the town was fortunate enough to have an endowed school (Plates 5 and 6). No register of the boys who attended it survives, and we cannot with certainty name a single one of the pupils. But since the school was there and the headmaster was paid, the easy and natural inference is that William Shakespeare was a pupil in it for some years—the easier because his father would have been at no expense for his tuition, for it was free for the sons of burgesses. The main subject at schools like Stratford's was Latin. By the time they had spent six or seven years there boys would have a pretty fair familiarity with considerable parts of Ovid, Virgil, Cicero, and Horace, and some acquaintance with other classical writers. The study of

Plate 4. Holy Trinity Church, Stratford. When William Shakespeare was carried to the baptismal font here on April 26, 1564, the church looked essentially as it now does, in its beautiful setting close beside the Avon. The central tower was built about 1200, the rest mainly a century and a half later.

rhetoric and of religion and morals, mostly conducted in the Latin tongue, was considered indispensable. A smattering of Greek was not uncommon. The supposition that Shakespeare's education was of this kind receives some support from the statement of Ben Jonson, a friend and fellow playwright, that he had "small Latin and less Greek"—an expression that must be judged in the light of Jonson's own extensive knowledge of the ancient languages, and in the light, too, of his well-known arrogance. The knowledge of Latin and of classical literature demonstrated in Shakespeare's plays and poems is not incompatible with the kind of education that an unusually bright boy might be expected to have acquired at the Stratford school.

The Stratford parish register contains no entry of Shakespeare's marriage, and from this we must suppose that it took place elsewhere. Ordinarily banns of matrimony were published in the parish church of the bride on three successive Sundays before a marriage. Marriage without banns or with one publication required a license from the bishop. Apparently Shakespeare, or someone on his behalf, applied to the Bishop of Worcester (in whose diocese Stratford lay) for such a license to marry Anne Hathaway. The record is not now complete: all that survives are an entry in the bishop's register stating that a license had been issued on November 27, 1582, and a bond, also in the bishop's registry and dated November 28, by which two sureties (both Stratford men) undertook that there was no legal impediment to the marriage, that it would not be carried out without the consent of the bride's relatives, and several other points. The bond stipulates one publication of the banns. Much puzzlement has been caused by the fact that in the entry the bride is called "Anna Whately of Temple Grafton" (a village near Stratford), while in the bond she is called "Anne Hathwey of Stratford." Careless confusion of two names by the clerk is the best explanation. William Shakespeare is named as the bridegroom in both documents. Anne—as we know from the inscription on her grave in Stratford—was eight years older than her husband.

The parish register supplies the next two dates. Under May 26, 1583 (six months after the date of the marriage license), is recorded the baptism of "Susanna daughter to William Shakespeare." The baptisms of two more children, twins, are recorded under date of February 2, 1585: "Hamnet & Judeth sonne and daughter to William Shakspere."

This is the last date for which there is any record of Shakespeare's being in Stratford until his return there some years later. We next hear of him as an actor and probably a playwright about 1592, when we can safely assume that he was living in London. Where was he in the interval of seven years or so? Many answers to this question have been proposed, all highly speculative, none supported by substantial evidence. The only possible answer is and must remain until new evidence is found, that we do not know. At some time after about the middle of the year 1584 Shakespeare left his native town and made his way, directly or indirectly, to London. As to the date of his departure we have not even the faintest clue. He may well have been, and indeed probably was, in London for a year or more before 1592, and there is no reason to suppose that he did not continue living in Stratford for some years after 1585.

Late in the year 1592 Robert Greene, a popular writer of plays, romances, and pamphlets, refers to Shakespeare in a pamphlet called *Greene's Groats-worth of Wit*. The passage as a whole is ambiguous, but in it Greene unmistakably quotes part of a line from *3 Henry VI* and speaks of Shakespeare as an actor. This play is not probably Shakespeare's first, and we must suppose that he did not become both actor and playwright overnight. Which play was his first is not known. Among the earliest were the three parts of *Henry VI, Richard III, The Comedy of Errors,* and *Titus Andronicus.* The last named of these was, in 1594, the first to appear in print—in a small unbound pamphlet, on the title-page of which the author is not named. His name was not, in fact, printed on the title-page of any play until 1598, when *Love's Labor's Lost* was said to be "By W.

Plate 5. The Grammar School. The upper room of the building on the left was used as the grammar school after the middle of the sixteenth century. Built about 1418, the building was originally the guildhall, and in Shakespeare's time the town council met in a room on the ground floor.

Plate 6. The Grammar School. This room has been in use as a schoolroom for some four hundred years. Here Shakespeare very probably learned his Latin.

12

Shakespere" and both *Richard II* and *Richard III* "By William Shake-speare." In this same year, 1598, a man named Francis Meres published a book called *Palladis Tamia: Wit's Treasury,* where, in a discussion of recent and living poets, he speaks of Shakespeare as enriching the English tongue with "rare ornaments and resplendent abiliments"; as "mellifluous and honeytongued Shakespeare"; as "among the English . . . the most excellent in both kinds"—both comedies and tragedies, he means, of which he names six each and thus provides a valuable gauge of the poet's early dramatic activity.

Meres also mentions Shakespeare as the author of *Venus and Adonis* and *The Rape of Lucrece.* By publishing the first of these in 1593 Shakespeare had established a reputation as a nondramatic poet. He dedicated it to Henry Wriothesley, Earl of Southampton, signing the dedication "William Shakespeare." *Lucrece* appeared in the following year, and the fact that it too is dedicated to the same nobleman suggests that the first dedication, as well as the first venture in nondramatic poetry, was well received. Beyond the existence of these two dedications nothing further is known about the relationship between the poet and his noble patron.

As actor and playwright Shakespeare was a member, at different times, of two or three acting companies. Every troupe of players had a patron—a nobleman, an important government official, or at least a man of influence. Bands of men wandering uncontrolled about the country were considered dangerous and were regarded with official suspicion. Since most troupes of actors subsisted by traveling from town to town and producing their plays in innyards and town halls, they fell under this suspicion and therefore required, on the one hand, the influence and protection effected by the license of a powerful patron and, on the other hand, his occasional restraint or discipline. London of course afforded the biggest audiences and the biggest profits, and it is natural that the best companies should have spent as much time there as possible. Before Shakespeare arrived on the

Plate 7. Clopton Bridge. In Roman times an important road, or "street," forded the Avon at Stratford, which got its name from that fact. Much later a wooden bridge was built here, and about 1500 Sir Hugh Clopton (the builder also of Shakespeare's house, New Place) built the present many-arched bridge of stone.

14

scene, several of these companies occupied, and in some cases controlled, newly erected permanent playhouses in London, the first ever built in England.

The years 1592 to 1594 are an obscure time in the history of the London stage. Severe outbreaks of the plague and other unsettling influences resulted in the dissolution of old acting companies and, in due course, the formation of new. Existing records are neither sufficiently complete nor sufficiently clear to throw much light on the dates or the composition of the several companies that operated in and out of London in the early nineties. With how many of these Shakespeare was connected as actor or as writer or both we cannot know. Two almost certainly were the Earl of Pembroke's company and the Earl of Sussex' company—commonly known for short as Pembroke's Men and Sussex' Men. It is possible too that during these years Shakespeare underwent at least one period of dramatic inactivity, which may have provided the opportunity or created the need for nondramatic writing. In 1594 the Lord Chamberlain's company was formed, and there is ample evidence of Shakespeare's connection with it from that year onward until his retirement, perhaps until his death. A record of a dramatic performance at the court of Queen Elizabeth in December 1594 names William Kemp, William Shakespeare, and Richard Burbage, "servants to the Lord Chamberlain." In the earlier companies to which he had been attached it is not unlikely that Shakespeare occupied a lowly position as a hired man, but there is some reason to believe that upon formation of the Chamberlain's Men he was from the first one of the sharers, or, as we should now put it, partners or stockholders. This is suggested by the inclusion of his name, as we have seen, with two of the chief members of the new company in its first recorded appearance at court.

So rapid a rise to prominence and importance in one of the leading theatrical companies must presumably mean that he was recognized by his fellows as possessing talents that would be of value to them. There being no testimony to his having shown

15

any notable superiority as an actor, we can only conclude that Shakespeare's services as a playwright were what the company valued. It is also possible that he was able to buy his share. A late tradition (Nicholas Rowe, 1709) has it that the Earl of Southampton rewarded him with £1,000 for the dedication of the two poems shortly before the formation of the Chamberlain's Men; the amount is utterly incredible (being the equivalent of something roughly like $50,000 today), but rich patrons were expected to give rewards, and a possible £100 would explain his ability to buy into the company. But this is conjecture: all we know is that Shakespeare appears to have been a leading member of the company from 1594 onward. In 1603 his name stands second in a list of nine sharers, a number which gradually increased in succeeding years of prosperity. In 1599 some seven of the sharers, Shakespeare being one, had built the Globe (Plates 8 and 9), the largest and most splendid of London playhouses, and in 1609 they expanded with the acquisition of a second house, a "private" indoor theatre, the Blackfriars. For this company, and only for it, Shakespeare wrote plays from the time of its foundation. Whether in addition he long continued as a regular actor it seems impossible to determine. Little significance can be attached to the fact that his name heads a list of the "Principall Actors in all these Playes" prefixed to the First Folio edition of his plays (1623).

Soon after James I came to the throne in 1603 the king himself took the company under his patronage, after which it was known as the King's Majesty's Servants, now usually the King's Men. The members were made Grooms of the Chamber, an honorary position in the royal household without fee, subsistence, or lodging. Ordinarily no duties were involved, but the Wardrobe accounts show the issue of scarlet cloth for liveries to "The Chamber," with the nine members of the acting company listed, Shakespeare's name first, in order that they might take part in a royal progress through London on March 15, 1604, to honor the Spanish Ambassador.

Shakespeare's position as a shareholder in the Lord Chamber-

Plate 8. The Globe Playhouse. This model was made by Dr. John Cranford Adams after exhaustive study of all the evidence. The nature of the evidence does not permit authoritative reconstruction of small details. Still, this model reliably represents the important features of the stage on which many of Shakespeare's plays were performed.

lain's company must be taken to explain the evidences of prosperity which begin to appear about 1596. It was in this year that his father—or he in his father's name—made a successful application to the College of Arms for the grant of a coat of arms. Such a grant constituted a step up in the world, one for which a minimum requisite was the possession of an income appropriate to the rank of gentleman, which rank, in theory at least, the grant conferred. John Shakespeare, who thirty years earlier had been mayor of Stratford and a man of worship and substance, had in recent years been suffering a steady decline in his business and his fortunes, connected, no doubt, with a general decline in the commerce of Stratford. Therefore it has usually been assumed, as in fact it was then by at least one man in a position to know, that the application for arms was actually initiated by the prosperous son. So long as the father was living the customary formalities of heraldry required that any grant of arms be to him rather than to a son.

Of Shakespeare's life in London aside from his plays and the theatre we have a few clear facts. From subsidy rolls we learn that he was assessed in October 1596 as a resident of St. Helen's parish, lying within the city wall in the north. Not far distant—just without the wall, through Bishopsgate—stood The Theatre, the playhouse principally occupied by the Chamberlain's Men during that period (Plate 9). Only a month or so later, on November 29, 1596, he had moved across the river to the Southwark side, where the Chamberlain's Men may now have occupied the new Swan playhouse. This information comes to us from a writ of attachment addressed to the sheriff of Surrey, charging William Shakespeare, Francis Langley, and two women with threatening bodily harm to one William Wayte. The sheriff of Surrey could attach only persons who lived in that county. Langley was the owner of the Swan, which stood on the south bank of the Thames, across the river from London proper and in Surrey. We do not know the precise nature of the quarrel between Wayte and the four persons of whom he demanded bonds requiring them to keep the peace, but the writ

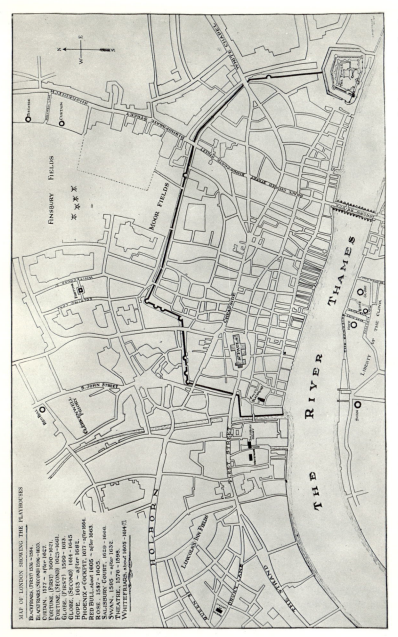

MAP OF LONDON SHOWING THE PLAYHOUSES

BLACKFRIARS, (FIRST) 1576 – 1584.
BLACKFRIARS, (SECOND) 1596 – 1655.
CURTAIN, 1577 – after 1627.
FORTUNE, (FIRST) 1600 – 1621.
FORTUNE, (SECOND) 1623 – 1661.
GLOBE, (FIRST) 1599 – 1613.
GLOBE, (SECOND) 1614 – 1645.
HOPE, 1613 – after 1682.
PHOENIX, or COCKPIT, 1617 – after 1664.
RED BULL, about 1605 – after 1663.
ROSE, 1587 – 1605.
SALISBURY COURT, 1629 – 1666.
SWAN, 1595 – after 1632.
THEATRE, 1576 – 1598.
WHITEFRIARS, about 1605 – 1614(?).

Plate 9. London. This rough map shows the positions of the playhouses—the Theatre (the first playhouse) north of the city on Bishopsgate Road, the Globe south across the Thames on the Bankside, and the others. The heavy black line represents the old city wall, the limit of municipal authority.

19

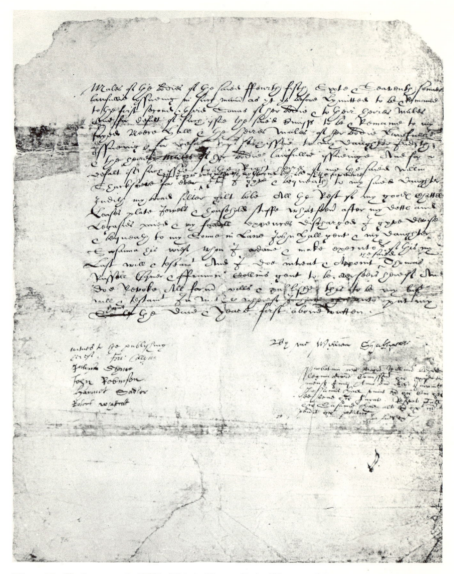

Plate 10. Shakespeare's Will, Third Sheet. Only "By me William Shakespeare" is in his own autograph. Sheets 1 and 2 are also signed, and these and three signatures on other documents are the only remaining specimens of Shakespeare's handwriting of which we can be perfectly sure. The will is in Somerset House, London.

20

of attachment well illustrates the way in which official archives can yield up biographical information. From another document, a deposition made by Shakespeare in a lawsuit of 1612, we learn that he, "William Shakespeare of Stratford upon Aven in the Countye of Warwicke gentleman of the age of xlviii yeres or thereaboutes," was, about 1602 and perhaps until 1604, lodging at the house of one Christopher Mountjoy, a French Huguenot tiremaker (a maker of fancy headdresses), in Cripplegate Ward, on the north side of the city. The fact that he is "of Stratford upon Aven" may be taken to indicate that he then had no London address but was settled in his native town.

It has usually been supposed that when Shakespeare went up to London he left his wife and children behind in Stratford. Though not improbable, this is not demonstrable, for all that we know with any degree of certainty is that Mrs. Shakespeare is never heard of in London, that the twins of 1585 were the last children known to have been born to her, that Hamnet, the only son, was buried in Stratford in 1596, and that the two daughters eventually married Stratford men. Shakespeare's *Sonnets,* probably written during the 1590's, have been thought to suggest a passionate attachment of the poet to a lady now unidentified. But this is guesswork, not fact, and the facts known hardly warrant the assumption of an estrangement between the poet and his wife. Shakespeare may from the beginning of his London career have kept in close touch with Stratford and his family, making frequent journeys thither.

Only after Shakespeare attained prosperity should we expect to find him buying real property and otherwise investing substantial sums, and this could scarcely have been before 1596, some two years after the formation of the Chamberlain's Men with Shakespeare as a sharer. The buying of New Place, one of the principal dwellings of Stratford, in 1597 certainly implies his presence in Stratford. From 1598 we have several letters which provide a glimpse of relations between Shakespeare and his fellow townsmen. Abraham Sturley, writing from Stratford to Richard Quiney (whose son was in a few years to marry Shakespeare's daughter Judith), speaks of property near the town which Shakespeare was considering buying and hopes he will also buy some of the Stratford tithes. In October of the same year Richard Quiney writes to Shakespeare from London, asking him to lend the considerable sum of £30 on security, and during the following month three other men of Stratford write to Quiney about this same money, apparently required for some important project. Shakespeare may have been in London at the time, but he was no stranger to his Stratford neighbors. From this time onward a number of investments and business transactions in and about Stratford suggest frequent visits there. In view of the inherent unlikelihood that all such transactions would be matters of record, it will be safe to assume that there were many more of them than we know of. In 1598 we find him dealing in malt—a common form of investment at that period in Warwickshire. In 1604 and again in 1608 he brought suit in the Stratford Court of Record for the recovery of money debts.

The purchase of New Place and other Stratford property suggests that even before the turn of the century Shakespeare began to think of the days when he might retire from the hurly-burly of city life to quiet domesticity among the rural scenes of his childhood. Not for some years yet was he to take such a step. Indeed in the first decade of the new century he was to reach his greatest dramatic activity and write his greatest plays. *Twelfth Night, Hamlet, Othello, King Lear, Macbeth,* and several others all belong to this period. This is the decade, too, in which the King's Men, now established in the new Globe, attained the first place among London acting companies. Prosperity came to Shakespeare about 1596; before his retirement he may have enjoyed some degree of wealth.

It was about 1610 or 1611 that he retired. Various reasons have been proposed by biographers: poor health, a yearning for a quiet life, a desire to be with his family, an inability to accommodate himself to the changing tastes of the playgoing public, who were beginning to demand novelty and psychological curiosity, to prefer tragicomedy to tragedy and comedy of manners to romantic comedy. We cannot know what motivated Shakespeare's decision—probably one of the considerations just mentioned, or a combination of them. There is reason for thinking, since they are not mentioned in his will, that he disposed of his shares in the King's Men and in their playhouses when he retired or soon after. His retirement from full participation in the company's affairs was not a clean break with London and the stage. He was pretty certainly in London on March 10, 1613, when he signed an indenture by which he bought a dwelling house there—formerly the gatehouse of what had been the Blackfriars Monastery. The price, £140, shows it to have been a rather substantial property. In June of the same year Shakespeare's company produced his last play, *Henry VIII* (thought by some authorities to have been written with a collaborator). What moved him to take up his pen again after a break of something like two years since he had written *The Tempest*, we do not know. An unhappy accident provided an ironic period to Shakespeare's stage career: during what may have been the first performance of *Henry VIII*, the shooting of a small cannon set the Globe playhouse on fire, and it burned to the ground.

On March 25, 1616, Shakespeare executed his will, the original of which, bearing his three signatures on its three sheets, has fortunately survived (Plate 10). The bulk of his estate, including New Place, the Blackfriars gatehouse, and other real property in and about Stratford, he left to his elder daughter Susanna. For his other daughter, Judith, who had married Thomas Quiney less than two months before the date of the will, he made provision by a substantial bequest of money. In addition he left several small bequests to other relatives and to a number of neighbors and friends—among the latter his "fellows" of the King's Men, John Heminges, Richard Burbage, and Henry Condell. These last bequests are of interest as demonstrating Shakespeare's close and lasting friendship with his professional associates, and especially the bequests to Heminges and Condell, because it was they who were, in 1623, to be in some

23

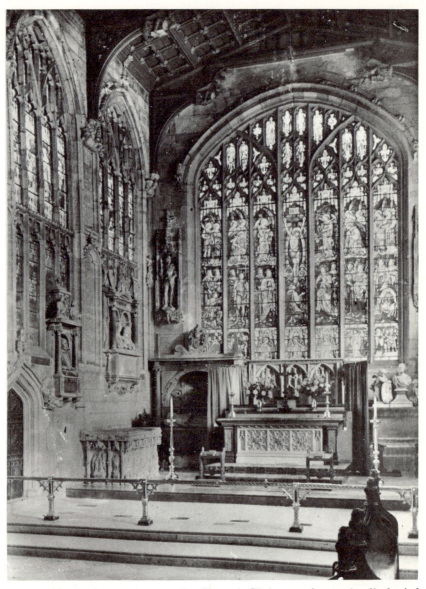

Plate 11. Holy Trinity Church, the Chancel. Shakespeare's remains lie buried under the floor of the sanctuary, inside the altar rail. Above, on the wall and in the window, just right of the door, is the memorial bust. This part of the church is perpendicular gothic of the late fifteenth century.

24

way responsible for the editing and publishing of Shakespeare's collected plays in the volume now commonly known as the First Folio (see Plate 14). This they did, they say, "only to keep the memory of so worthy a friend and fellow alive as was our Shakespeare." The will mentions Shakespeare's wife only in a single bequest inserted between the lines as if it were an afterthought, leaving to her his "second best bed." No significance is to be attached to this. With or without a will, she was by common law protected in her rights of dower to a life interest in any portions of the estate not specifically exempted, and these would have given her a comfortable income and the right to occupy New Place during her life. Both the substance and the form of the bequest may be plausibly accounted for by supposing that Mrs. Shakespeare asked for the bed.

Just under a month later, on April 23, 1616, Shakespeare died, probably within a day or two of the birthday on which he would have been fifty-two years old. The shortness of the interval between Shakespeare's will and his death has naturally led to the assumption that illness and the expectation of an early death led to the making of the will. Some persons have claimed to see further evidence of illness in the signatures. While such illness cannot be regarded as altogether improbable, there is in fact no evidence of it. There is nothing odd about the signatures; they were originally quite firm and are now as clear and legible as the state of the paper permits. The timing of the will is sufficiently accounted for by Shakespeare's desire to make suitable provision for his daughter Judith in view of her recent (and belated) marriage. We can safely assume that it was for this reason that a new will was substituted for one made much earlier. The only seventeenth-century account of Shakespeare's death suggests that it was sudden. John Ward, vicar of Stratford from 1662 to 1681, wrote in a notebook, "Shakespear, Drayton, and Ben Jhonson had a merry meeting, and itt seems drank too hard, for Shakespear died of a feavour there contracted." This John Ward kept notes on many subjects, chiefly medical and theological, in calf-bound notebooks, of which sixteen have

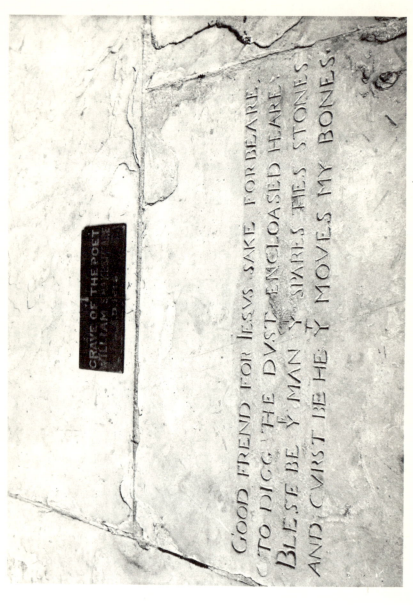

GOOD FREND FOR IESVS SAKE FORBEARE,
TO DIGG THE DVST ENCLOASED HEARE.
BLESE BE Y MAN Y SPARES HES STONES,
AND CVRST BE HE Y MOVES MY BONES.

GRAVE OF THE POET
WILLIAM SHAKESPEARE
D. 1616

Plate 12. Shakespeare's Epitaph. This floor slab marks the grave in the chancel of Holy Trinity Church. Tradition has it that Shakespeare composed the crude epitaph, and this, if not probable, is at least possible. Nearby in the chancel are also buried Shakespeare's wife, his daughter Susanna, and her husband John Hall.

survived (and are now in the Folger Library). He had studied medicine and appears to have been a cautious and intelligent man much interested in Stratford antiquities. Though his report is hearsay, still it is hearsay well founded: Ward was in a position to know the truth, for the facts would have been widely talked about at the time of the poet's death, and many persons who might have attended the funeral must still have been alive in Stratford when Ward made his entry in a volume dated 1661–1663. Nevertheless, we can accept the story only with reservations, as a plausible account which conflicts with no other evidence.

Shakespeare's remains were interred under the floor of the chancel of Holy Trinity Church, the parish church of Stratford, just inside the altar rail. The well-known epitaph carved in a floor stone (Plate 12) has been attributed to Shakespeare himself, and, rude doggerel though it be, there is no serious bar to our accepting this attribution. The obvious purpose of the epitaph is to frighten off anyone planning to disturb the grave, and it is not difficult to conceive that Shakespeare, who always knew how to suit poetic style to his auditory and his purpose, would here pitch his verse to the level of gravediggers and the like. In any case, the epitaph has been successful, for the grave has never been opened or disturbed. At some time between 1616 and 1622 a monument was erected on the north wall of the chancel, not far from the gravestone (Plate 13). Executed by Garratt Janssen, a Flemish tomb maker of Southwark and one of the best of his trade, the monument is of superior workmanship and is characteristic of the artist and of the time. In spite of its obviously conventional and stylized portraiture, M. H. Spielmann, the leading authority on the subject, thinks it probable that it was based on a life mask. However this may be, the "Stratford bust" must be regarded as an informed attempt to represent the poet's appearance with some fidelity. The 1623 First Folio edition of the plays contains a copperplate portrait, probably made from a drawing or miniature and probably showing Shakespeare at an early age (Plate 14). It is crudely

Plate 13. The Memorial Bust, Holy Trinity Church. This monument, of painted limestone, almost certainly executed by Garratt Janssen, a London tomb maker, was erected before 1623. It is of stylized design conventional in that period and of good quality. The trouble and expense thus willingly incurred by a survivor are some guarantee that pains would have been taken to obtain a reasonable likeness of the poet.

designed and has generally been regarded with disapproval, but it is quite evidently a portrait of the same man represented in the Stratford monument. Except for these two, executed soon after Shakespeare's death, no other portrait can be shown to have originated before about 1675 or to possess the slightest authority as a faithful delineation of Shakespeare's face.

He was survived by his two daughters and one granddaughter. Susanna had married Dr. John Hall, a Stratford physician, and they had a daughter Elizabeth, born in 1608. Judith was but newly married to Thomas Quiney. In his will, as we have seen, Shakespeare left all of his real property, the bulk of his estate, to his elder daughter, putting into the will an entail apparently designed to ensure the descent of this considerable estate in the male line of the Hall family. If he saw himself as the progenitor of a long line of substantial propertied descendants, his dream was destined to be thwarted. Elizabeth was the Halls' only child, and she, though twice married, died childless in 1670. The Quineys made a better start with three sons, but they died young and unmarried, the last in 1639. But if Shakespeare was denied a line of descendants, he left, in his plays, a progeny which will keep his memory fresh while civilization lasts.

MR. WILLIAM

SHAKESPEARES

COMEDIES,
HISTORIES, &
TRAGEDIES.

Published according to the True Originall Copies.

LONDON
Printed by Isaac Iaggard, and Ed. Blount. 1623.

Plate 14. The First Folio Title-Page. The first edition of Shakespeare's collected plays was prepared with the assistance of two of his friends and fellow actors. The engraved portrait, if somewhat crude, is clearly a representation of the same man shown in the memorial bust at Stratford and must have been approved by his friends.

SUGGESTED READING

Sir Edmund K. Chambers, *William Shakespeare: A Study of Facts and Problems* (2 vols., Oxford, 1930) is the most complete and reliable biography, containing transcripts of all the important documents but because of its closely compressed style is not easy reading.

Joseph Quincy Adams, *A Life of William Shakespeare* (Boston and New York, 1923), though now somewhat out-of-date, is both readable and accurate and is reliable except where more recent scholarship has superseded it.

Hazelton Spencer, *The Art and Life of William Shakespeare* (New York, [1940]) is an excellent life with emphasis on the plays, reliable when dealing with fact, weak in criticism and interpretation; it contains valuable information on stage history, Spencer's specialty.

Marchette Chute, *Shakespeare of London* (New York, 1949) is a biography both easy and pleasant to read, the best of its kind, in which accuracy is not sacrificed to the desire to produce a popular work.

F. E. Halliday, *Shakespeare: A Pictorial Biography* (London, [1956]) contains scores of excellent and well-chosen pictures of Stratford, London, the playhouses, the early books, the manuscripts and records, with brief text.

F. E. Halliday, *A Shakespeare Companion, 1550–1950* (London, [1952]) is a useful dictionary of concise information on Shakespeare's life, his environment, his plays, and the publication, criticism, and production of his plays.

Shakespeare's England: An Account of the Life and Manners of His Age (2 vols., Oxford, 1917) consists of chapters (each by a different authority) on the court, education, agriculture, law, the sciences, the fine arts, sports and pastimes, and other subjects; though now somewhat out-of-date, it is an extremely valuable storehouse of information.

Sir Edmund K. Chambers, *The Elizabethan Stage* (4 vols., Oxford, 1923) presents an exhaustive study of the playhouses and acting companies, 1550–1616, with valuable appendixes listing plays, dramatists, etc.; it is superseded at some points by more recent scholarship and is not easy reading.

Virgil K. Whitaker, *Shakespeare's Use of Learning* (San Marino, Calif., 1953) consists of a thorough examination of Shakespeare's sources and the reading which influenced him; Chapters 1 and 2 contain valuable discussion of his education.

Marion H. Spielmann, *The Title-page of the First Folio of Shakespeare's Plays: A Comparative Study of the Droeshout Portrait and the Stratford Monument* (London, 1924) presents the most authoritative discussion of the early portraiture of the poet.

William Jaggard, *Shakespeare Bibliography* (Stratford, 1911) achieves a remarkable degree of success in an attempt to list every edition (in English) of Shakespeare's writings and every work about him or related to him up to 1910.

Walther Ebisch and Levin L. Schücking, *A Shakespeare Bibliography* (2 vols., Oxford, 1931) lists important works on Shakespeare, arranged under subject headings.